MW01608511

# Chinese Flash Cards

## 186 Essential Chinese Characters
## For Beginners

| 一 | 二 |
|---|---|
| 三 | 四 |
| 五 | 六 |

**èr**
*two*

**yī**
*one*

**sì**
*four*

**sān**
*three*

**liù**
*six*

**wǔ**
*five*

Card 1

七　八

九　零

十　百

**bā**
*eight*

**qī**
*seven*

**líng**
*zero*

**jiǔ**
*nine*

**bǎi**
*hundred*

**shí**
*ten*

Card 2

| 千 | 万 |
| 亿 | 两 |
| 我 | 你 |

**wàn**
*ten thousand*

**qiān**
*thousand*

**liǎng**
*both (few)*

**yì**
*hundred million*

**nǐ**
*you*

**wǒ**
*I*

Card 3

您　他

她　它

谁　个

**tā**
*he*

**nín**
*you (formal)*

**tā**
*it*

**tā**
*she*

**gè**
*individual / piece / universal measure word*

**shéi**
*who*

Card 4

| | |
|---|---|
| 岁 | 本 |
| 些 | 块 |
| 不 | 没 |

## běn
*roots or stems of plants / origin / source / this / the current / root / foundation / basis / (a measure word)*

## suì
*year / years old / (a measure word)*

## kuài
*piece / chunk / lump / (measure word for chunks, lumps)*

## xiē
*some / few / several / (a measure word)*

## méi
*have not / not*

## bù
*not / no*

Card 5

| | |
|---|---|
| 很 | 太 |
| 都 | 和 |
| 与 | 给 |

**tài**
*highest / greatest / too (much) / very / extremely*

**hěn**
*very*

**hé**
*and / together with / with*

**dōu**
*all*

**gěi**
*to / for / for the benefit of / to give / to allow / to do sth (for sb) / (passive particle)*

**yǔ**
*and / to give / together with*

Card 6

| | |
|---|---|
| 跟 | 在 |
| 前 | 后 |
| 右 | 左 |

**zài**
*(located)*
*at / in / exist*

**gēn**
*to follow / to go with*
*/ heel / with /*
*and*

**hòu**
*(space) back / behind / rear*
*(time) afterwards / after /*
*later/ last*

**qián**
*before / in front / ago /*
*former / previous / earlier /*
*front*

**zuǒ**
*left*

**yòu**
*right (-hand)*

Card 7

的　了

吗　呢

为　位

**le**

*(modal particle intensifying preceding clause) / (completed action marker)*

**de**

*(possessive particle) / of*

**ne**

*(question particle)*

**mǎ**

*morphine*

**wèi**

*position / location / (measure word for persons) / place / seat*

**wéi**

*act as*

Card 8

| 喂 | 这 |
|---|---|
| 哪 | 那 |
| 家 | 几 |

**zhè**
*this / these*

**wéi**
*(interjection) hello / to feed (someone or some animal) / hey / telephone greeting*

**nà**
*that / those*

**nǎ**
*how / which*

**jǐ**
*a few / how many how much / several / a few*

**jiā**
*family, home*

Card 9

火　　车

站　　中

国　　面

# chē
*car / a vehicle / machine*

# huǒ
*fire*

# zhōng
*middle, center*

# zhàn
*station*

# miàn
*fade / side / surface / aspect / top / face / flour / noodles / flour / noodles*

# guó
*country / state / nation*

Card 10

期　时

去　来

下　上

**shí**
*O'clock / time*

**qī**
*a period of time*

**lái**
*to come*

**qù**
*to go*

**shàng**
*on / on top / upon / first (of two parts) / previous or last (week, etc.) / upper / higher / above / previous / to climb / to go into / above / to go up*

**xià**
*under / second (of two parts) / next (week, etc.) / lower / below*

| 里 | 外 |
|---|---|
| 钱 | 次 |
| 词 | 此 |

**wài**
*outside / in addition / foreign / external*

**lǐ**
*inside / internal / interior*

**cì**
*number (of times) / order / sequence / next / second(ary) / (measure word)*

**qián**
*money*

**cǐ**
*this / these*

**cí**
*words / phrases*

Card 12

天　日

月　年

点　分

# rì
*day / sun / date / day of the month*

# tiān
*day / sky / heaven*

# nián
*year*

# yuè
*moon / month*

# fēn
*to divide / minute / (a measure word) / (a unit of length = 0.33 centimeter)*

# diǎn
*o'clock / (a measure word) / point / dot / (decimal) point)*

秒　电

爸　妈

第　弟

**diàn**
*electric / electricity / electrical*

**miǎo**
*(a measure word) / second*

**mā**
*mother*

**bà**
*father*

**dì**
*younger brother*

**dì**
*(prefix before a number, for ordering numbers, e.g. "first", "number two", etc)*

哥　美

街　妹

每　姐

**měi**
*beautiful*

**gē**
*elder brother*

**mèi**
*younger sister*

**jiē**
*street*

**jiě**
*older sister*

**měi**
*each / every*

Card 15

| | |
|:-:|:-:|
| 节 | 老 |
| 大 | 小 |
| 多 | 少 |

**lǎo**
*old*

**jié**
*festival / section / segment / point / part / to economize / to save / temperate*

**xiǎo**
*small / tiny / few / young*

**dà**
*big / huge / large*

**shǎo**
*few / little / lack*

**duō**
*many / much / a lot of*

Card 16

| | |
|---|---|
| 女 | 男 |
| 难 | 贵 |
| 鬼 | 南 |

| | |
|---|---|
| **nán**<br>*male* | **nǚ**<br>*female / woman* |
| **guì**<br>*expensive* | **nán**<br>*difficult* |
| **nán**<br>*South* | **guǐ**<br>*ghost* |

Card 17

| | |
|---|---|
| 北 | 西 |
| 东 | 园 |
| 元 | 远 |

| | |
|---|---|
| **xī**<br>*West* | **běi**<br>*North* |
| **yuán**<br>*garden* | **dōng**<br>*East* |
| **yuǎn**<br>*far* | **yuán**<br>*(Chinese currency)* |

Card 18

| 近 | 金 |
| 进 | 出 |
| 口 | 水 |

**jīn**
*metal / money / gold*

**jìn**
*near*

**chū**
*to go out / come out / leave*

**jìn**
*enter / to come in*

**shuǐ**
*water*

**kǒu**
*mouth / (a measure word)*

书　米

树　菜

费　非

Back

**mǐ**
*(measure word)*
*meter / rice*

**shū**
*book*

**cài**
*dish (type of food) /*
*vegetables*

**shù**
*tree*

**fēi**
*non- / not- / un-*

**fèi**
*to cost / to spend / fee /*
*wasteful / expenses*

Card 20

| 飞 | 表 |
|---|---|
| 手 | 受 |
| 帽 | 猫 |

**biǎo**
*to show,*
*outside, surface*

**fēi**
*to fly*

**shòu**
*to receive*

**shǒu**
*hand*

**māo**
*cat*

**mào**
*hat / cap*

Card 21

毛　够

狗　人

名　雪

| | |
|---|---|
| **gòu**<br>*enough* | *máo*<br>*hair / pore / fur* |
| **rén**<br>*man / person / people* | **gǒu**<br>*dog* |
| **xuě**<br>*snow* | **míng**<br>*name / (measure word for persons) / place (e.g. among winners)* |

Card 22

鞋 写

谢 鱼

雨 语

**xiě**
*to write*

**xié**
*shoe*

**yú**
*fish*

**xiè**
*to thank*

**yǔ**
*language / speech*

**yǔ**
*rain*

Card 23

| | |
|---|---|
| 热 | 冷 |
| 再 | 才 |
| 有 | 又 |

**lěng**
*cold*

**rè**
*hot*

**cái**
*ability / talent / endowment /
gift / an expert / only (then) /
only if / just
just / not until*

**zài**
*again*

*yòu*
*(once) again*

**yǒu**
*to have*

Card 24

| | |
|---|---|
| 油 | 是 |
| 看 | 听 |
| 说 | 读 |

**shì**
*to be / yes*

**yóu**
*oil / sly*

**tīng**
*to listen / to hear / to obey*

**kān**
*to look after / to take care of / to watch*

**dú**
*to read / to study*

**shuō**
*to speak / to say*

| 叫 | 回 |
|---|---|
| 会 | 能 |
| 吃 | 课 |

**huí**

*to return, to go back*

**jiào**

*to (be) call(ed)*

**néng**

*can / may / capable / energy / able*

**huì**

*can / be possible / be able to*

**kè**

*subject / class / lesson*

**chī**

*to eat*

Card 26

| 喝 | 打 |
| 坐 | 买 |
| 卖 | 祝 |

**dǎ**
*to beat / to strike / to break / to mix up / to build / to fight*

**hē**
*to drink*

**mǎi**
*to buy*

**zuò**
*to sit*

**zhù**
*to wish*

**mài**
*to sell*

Card 27

| | |
|---|---|
| 做 | 住 |
| 楼 | 开 |
| 爱 | 像 |

**zhù**
*to live*

**zuò**
*to do / to make / to produce*

**kāi**
*to open / to operate (vehicle) / to start*

**lóu**
*house with more than 1 story / storied building / floor*

**xiàng**
*to (look) like / similar (to)*

**ài**
*to love*

Card 28

| | |
|---|---|
| 要 | 想 |
| 药 | 号 |
| 高 | 好 |

**xiǎng**

*to think / to believe / to suppose / to wish / to want / to miss*

**yāo**

*to demand / to ask / to request*

**hào**

*day of a month / (suffix used after) name of a ship / (ordinal) number*

**yào**

*medicine / drug / cure*

**hǎo**

*good / well*

**gāo**

*high / tall*

Card 29

| | |
|:---:|:---:|
| 地 | 低 |
| 亮 | 古 |
| 未 | 未 |

**dī**
*low*

**dì**
*earth / ground / field / place / land*

**gǔ**
*ancient / old*

**liàng**
*light / bright*

**mò**
*end / final stage / latter part*

**wèi**
*not*

Card 30

| 湖 | 河 |
| 饿 | 海 |
| 洋 | 死 |

| | |
|---|---|
| **hé**<br>*river* | *hú*<br>*lake* |
| **hǎi**<br>*ocean / sea* | **è**<br>*to be hungry / hungry /*<br>*to starve (somebody)* |
| **sǐ**<br>*to die* | **yáng**<br>*ocean* |

Card 31

Made in the USA
Middletown, DE
09 December 2021

54982447R00038